If you were a

Pronoun

by Nancy Loewen
illustrated by Sara Gray

PICTURE WINDOW BOOKS
Minneapolis, Minnesota

pronoun **(pron)** a word that
takes the place of a noun

Editor: Christianne Jones
Designer: Tracy Kaehler
Page Production: Lori Bye
Creative Director: Keith Griffin
Editorial Director: Carol Jones
The illustrations in this book
were created with acrylics.

Picture Window Books
5115 Excelsior Boulevard
Suite 232
Minneapolis, MN 55416
877-845-8392
www.picturewindowbooks.com

Printed in the United States of America.

**Library of Congress
Cataloging-in-Publication Data**
Loewen, Nancy, 1964–
If you were a pronoun / by Nancy Loewen; illustrated
by Sara Gray.
p. cm. — (Word fun)
Includes bibliographical references.
ISBN-13: 978-1-4048-2637-3 (hardcover)
ISBN-10: 1-4048-2637-8 (hardcover)
ISBN-13: 978-1-4048-2639-7 (paperback)
ISBN-10: 1-4048-2639-4 (paperback)
1. English language—Pronoun—Juvenile literature. I. Gray,
Sara, ill. II. Title. III. Series.
PE1261.L56 2006
428.2—dc22   2006003396

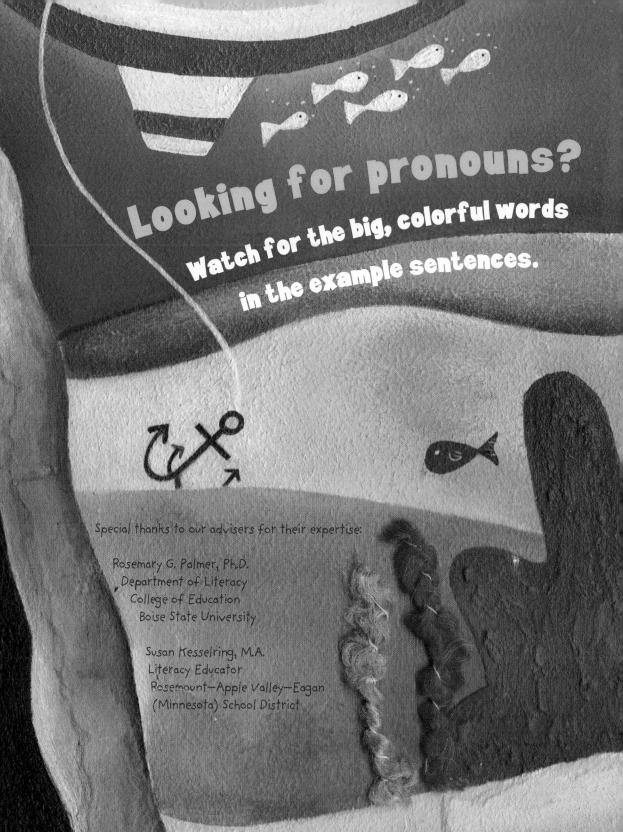

Looking for pronouns?

Watch for the big, colorful words

in the example sentences.

Special thanks to our advisers for their expertise:

Rosemary G. Palmer, Ph.D.
Department of Literacy
College of Education
Boise State University

Susan Kesselring, M.A.
Literacy Educator
Rosemount–Apple Valley–Eagan
(Minnesota) School District

If you were
a pronoun ...

... **YOU** could throw a party. **YOU** would invite

HIM and **HER** and **THEM** and **US**.

4

YOU would invite **EVERYBODY!**

"Come ONE, come ALL,"
YOU would say.
"WE will have a
terrific time!"

5

If you were a pronoun, you would replace nouns and take the repetition out of sentences.

Without Pronouns

Jessie put Jessie's backpack in Jessie's locker. Then Jessie went to talk to Jessie's friends.

With Pronouns

Jessie put **HER** backpack in **HER** locker. Then **SHE** went to talk to **HER** friends.

7

If you were a pronoun, you could take the place of more than one person or thing.

Carol, Bruce, and I earned a pizza party for the entire class.

WE earned a pizza party for the entire class.

8

Frank and Dylan each ate three slices of pizza. THEY each ate three slices of pizza.

9

If you were a pronoun, you could take the place of a person or a person's name. You would be a personal pronoun.

Mrs. Jones handed out the tests.

SHE handed out the tests.

10

Brian was nervous for the test.

HE was nervous for the test.

If you were a pronoun, you could be possessive. You would let people know that something belongs to someone or something.

Sharky lost some of **HIS** teeth.

OUR playground equipment needs to be cleaned.

If you were a pronoun, you could tell about people and things without being specific. You would be an indefinite pronoun.

EVERYONE get ready to march.

Did I forget **SOMETHING?**

I don't want to trip over **ANYTHING**.

SOMEBODY lost some sheet music.

Other common indefinite pronouns include SOMEONE, ALL, ANYONE, NO ONE, ANY, EVERYBODY, NONE, SEVERAL, SOME, BOTH, NEITHER, NOBODY, NOTHING, and MANY.

If you were a pronoun, you could ask questions.
You would be an interrogative pronoun.

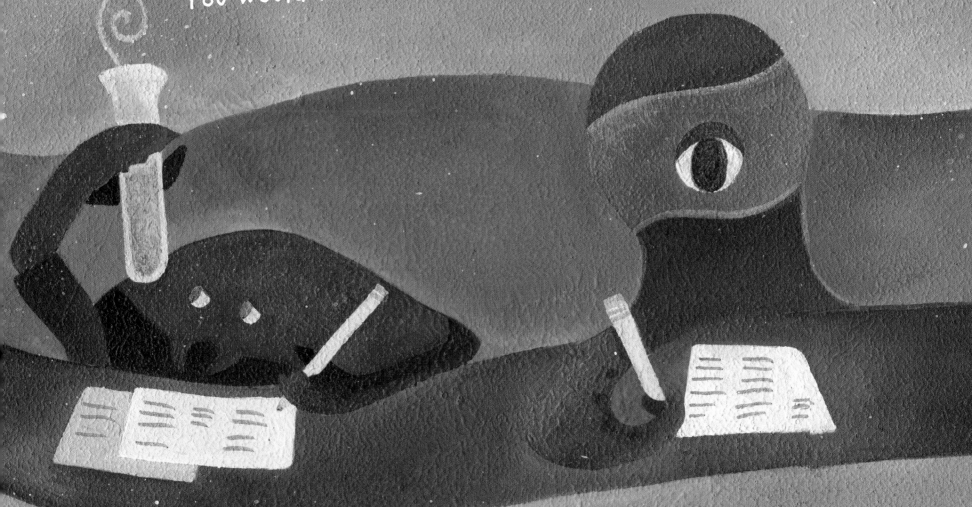

WHAT is in here?

WHO understands this stuff?

16

WHICH is the right one?

WHOM and WHOSE are other interrogative pronouns.

If you were a pronoun, you could point something out without naming it. You would be a demonstrative pronoun.

Please give me THOSE.

I'll take THESE.

If you were a pronoun, you could be like a mirror. You could reflect the subject of the sentence back to itself. The subject tells whom or what the sentence is about.

I can fix it **MYSELF**.

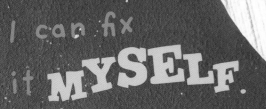

THEY will get **THEMSELVES** into a lot of trouble if THEY eat THEIR textbooks!

If you were a pronoun, you could emphasize the subject of the sentence.

The principal **HERSELF** decorated the set for the school play.

21

You would always
be working hard
as a stand-in ...

... if you were
a pronoun!

22

Fun with Pronouns

Gather some friends and some old newspaper or magazine articles.

Give each player a highlighter or a bright crayon.

When someone says go, quickly read through your articles, marking every pronoun you see.

Try doing this for one minute. After one minute, the player with the most pronouns wins.

Fact: If you look up a pronoun in the dictionary, you will see the abbreviation "pron" next to it. The "pron" stands for pronoun.

23

Glossary

demonstrative pronoun—a type of pronoun that helps point
something out without naming it
emphasize—to give more importance to something
indefinite pronoun—a type of pronoun that tells about people and
things without being specific
interrogative pronoun—a type of pronoun that asks a question
nouns—words that name a person, place, or thing
personal pronoun—a type of pronoun that takes the place of a person
possessive pronoun—a type of pronoun that shows that an object
belongs to someone or something
reflect—to throw back
repetition—to repeat
subject—a word or group of words in a sentence that tells
whom or what the sentence is about

To Learn More

At the Library
Cleary, Brian P. *I and You and Don't Forget Who: What
  Is a Pronoun?* Minneapolis: Carolrhoda Books, 2004.
Heinrichs, Ann. *Pronouns.* Chanhassen, Minn.:
  Child's World, 2004.
Heller, Ruth. *Mine, All Mine: A Book About Pronouns.*
  New York: Puffin Books, 1999.

On the Web
FactHound offers a safe, fun way to find Web
sites related to this book. All of the sites on
FactHound have been researched by our staff.

1. Visit *www.facthound.com*
2. Type in this special
  code: 1404826378
3. Click on the FETCH IT button.

Your trusty FactHound will fetch the best sites for you!